To the Reader . . .

The **Raintree/Rivilo American Indian Stories** series features the lives of American Indian men and women important in the history of their tribes. Our purpose is to provide young readers with accurate accounts of the lives of these individuals. The stories are written by scholars, including American Indians.

Indians are as much a part of American life today as they were one hundred years ago. Even in times past, Indians were not all the same. Not all of them lived in tepees or wore feather warbonnets. They were not all warriors. Some did fight against the white man, but many befriended him.

Whether patriot or politician, athlete or artist, Arapaho or Zuni, the story of each person in this series deserves to be told. Whether the individuals gained distinction on the battlefield or the playing field, in the courtroom or the classroom, they have enriched the heritage and history of all Americans. It is hoped that those who read their stories will realize that many different peoples, regardless of culture or color, have played a part in shaping the United States, in making America the great country that it is today.

Herman J. Viola
General Editor
Author of Exploring the West
and others on the West
and

GENERAL EDITOR

Herman J. Viola

Author of *Exploring the West* and other volumes on the West
and American Indians

MANAGING EDITOR

Robert M. Kvasnicka

Coeditor of *The Commissioners of Indian Affairs, 1824-1977*
Coeditor of *Indian-White Relations: A Persistent Paradox*

MANUSCRIPT EDITOR

Barbara J. Behm

DESIGNER

Kathleen A. Hartnett

PRODUCTION

Andrew Rupniewski
Eileen Rickey

Library of Congress Number: 89-10411

1 2 3 4 5 6 7 8 9   95 94 93 92 91 90 89

Library of Congress Cataloging-in-Publication Data

Kvasnicka, Robert M.
  Hole-in-the-Day.
  (Raintree American Indian stories)
  Summary: A biography of Hole-in-the-Day, chief of the
Mississippi bands of the Chippewa in Minnesota, who was known
for his intelligence, bravery, and oratory skills.
  1. Hole-in-the-Day, Chief, 1828-1868—Juvenile literature.
2. Ojibwa Indians—Biography—Juvenile literature. 3. Indians of
North America—Minnesota—Biography—Juvenile literature.
[1. Hole-in-the-Day, Chief, 1828-1868. 2. Ojibwa Indians—
Biography. 3. Indians of North America—Biography] I. Title.
II. Series.
E99.C6H645 1989   977.6'00497302   [B] [92]   89-10411
ISBN 0-8172-3405-5 (lib. bdg.)

AMERICAN INDIAN STORIES

HOLE-IN-THE-DAY

Text by Robert M. Kvasnicka
Illustrations by Rick Whipple

Raintree Publishers
Milwaukee

Hole-in-the-Day was only nineteen years old when he became an important leader of the Chippewa tribe in Minnesota. This very intelligent young man led his people when they sold their lands to the United States government and moved onto reservations that still exist today. Because Hole-in-the-Day was an able leader, the Chippewa still live in areas where they lived when the white settlers came to Minnesota. Hole-in-the-Day believed in following the white man's way of life. He became a farmer and lived in a fine house. He served meals on china dishes and subscribed to newspapers that were read to him by his personal interpreter.

Long before they came to Minnesota, the Chippewa, also called the Ojibwa, Indians lived near the mouth of the St. Lawrence River in Canada. Gradually they moved westward. By the mid-1700s, they were pushing the Sioux out of the area around the headwaters of the Mississippi River. For the next one hundred years, the Chippewa and the Sioux fought each other for the right to live in Minnesota's forests.

In the early 1820s, the United States government built Fort Snelling to provide the white settlers with protection from the warring tribes. The fort still stands on the outskirts of the Twin Cities of Minneapolis and St. Paul. A government Indian agent lived at the fort. His job was to try to keep peace between the Chippewa and the Sioux, but he had little success. From the continuing warfare came two colorful and exciting Chippewa leaders, Hole-in-the-Day and his father, who was also called Hole-in-the-Day.

The younger Hole-in-the-Day (Pug-o-ne-ge-shick) was born about 1828 near Sandy Lake in northern Minnesota. His father was an ambitious and proud warrior. His mother was the daughter of Broken Tooth, an important Chippewa chief. They called their baby Kwi-wi-sens, or Boy.

Boy grew up in a land that was filled with trees, dotted with lakes, and crisscrossed with rivers. From the trees the Chippewa got wood for their tools, their utensils, and their weapons. Tree bark was used as a covering for their wigwam homes and on their canoes. The forest was also home for deer, moose, and other game that provided the Chippewa with food and hides for clothing. The lakes and rivers were a source of food also. Wild rice grew along the lakeshores, and fish were plentiful. The waterways were used as highways by the Chippewa whose main means of travel was the canoe.

Little is known about Boy's early years. He probably was raised in the traditional Chippewa way. As a baby, he spent much of his time strapped to a cradleboard by a buckskin wrapping that his mother decorated with quills or beads. When he was older, he learned how to fish and trap, and how to hunt with a bow and arrow. When he killed his first game, perhaps a rabbit or maybe even a deer, the family held a small celebration called the Feast for the First Kill. His father also taught him that he was a member of an important family. He should always try to be the best at all he did.

The most important event in any Indian boy's life was his vision quest. Chippewa boys usually spent about four days alone in the forest. They ate no food so that they would dream at night. The things they dreamed about would guide them for the rest of their lives. The dreams gave them a guardian spirit that they would always look to for help and protection.

By the time he reached the age when most Indian boys had their vision quest, Boy already had earned the right to wear an eagle feather in his hair. This meant that he had killed an enemy. When Boy was nine, the Sioux had murdered several Chippewa, including Boy's stepbrother and two other relatives. Boy's father was very angry. Because he had worked with the government for fifteen years to keep peace with the Sioux, however, he hid his real feelings and took no steps to avenge the deaths.

In the following spring, he took Boy and several other Chippewa to join some Sioux in a hunting trip. That evening one of the Sioux angered Boy's father whose patience finally snapped. Later that night, he and his men, including Boy, killed three Sioux men, four women, and four children.

Boy's father soon was sorry the Sioux families had been killed, but he had several more bloody fights with the Sioux before he died.

Despite his success as a warrior, Boy's father had grown tired of the continual warfare. He knew that the Chippewa's traditional way of life was vanishing. His people had to learn to get along with the whites. He wanted peace so his people could learn how to farm and live like their white neighbors. He wanted Boy, who would be the Chippewa's future leader, to be educated like white children. Several times he asked for a missionary to be sent to his people to start a school, but his requests were ignored. Boy was educated through experience rather than formal schooling.

Boy's father died in 1847. By that time, he had become head chief over all the bands of the Mississippi Chippewa. The band chiefs accepted him because he was a great leader. He had kept them at peace with the whites. His bravery and daring had given them many victories over the Sioux. Before he died, he told Boy to lead the tribe and to "make them resemble the whites." Although Boy was only nineteen, he intended to do just that. The first thing he did was to take his father's name. From then on, he called himself Hole-in-the-Day.

That summer the government called the Indians together for a treaty council. Young Hole-in-the-Day immediately took charge. He told the government officials that he was now head chief and that he would speak for all the Chippewa. The older chiefs were amazed at his boldness. The white officials were impressed by his behavior. They all accepted his claim to leadership.

Hole-in-the-Day was a very charming and handsome young man. He had several wives, possibly as many as four at one time. He was at his most charming one day in June 1850. He and some of his men were at Fort Snelling to hold a peace conference with the Sioux. Many people who lived near the fort came to see what would happen when the two tribes met. The Sioux, who were insulted because women were in the crowd, walked out of the council. Hole-in-the-Day welcomed the women, but they decided to leave so that the Sioux would return to the council. Hole-in-the-Day shook hands with each woman as she left.

The winter of 1850-1851 was very hard on the Chippewa. Many Indians were dying from hunger and the cold. Hole-in-the-Day looked for some way to help them. Because he was known for his exciting speeches, he invited the members of the Minnesota Territorial Legislature and other important townspeople to hear him speak at a church in St. Paul. He told them how hard life was for his people and how much they were suffering. His musical voice, commanding manner, and passionate delivery held his audience spellbound. Even though his words had to be translated into English, the people were deeply moved by his emotional plea for their help. They set up a committee to collect money for the Chippewa.

In January 1855, Hole-in-the-Day and other Chippewa leaders were called to Washington, D.C., to make a new treaty. The Chippewa dealt with Commissioner of Indian Affairs George W. Manypenny, who directed Indian policy for President Franklin Pierce. The government hoped to buy ten million acres of Chippewa land. Hole-in-the-Day was not happy with the terms offered. He wanted some things that the commissioner could not give. For example, he thought that the Chippewa should be made citizens of the United States. Then they would be treated as well as white men and they would have the right to vote. More realistically, Hole-in-the-Day wanted his people to learn the ways of the whites. An agreement was finally made, but Hole-in-the-Day still thought that the Chippewa had not received enough money for their land. For about fourteen cents an acre, the government had bought much of northern Minnesota including Lake Itasca, the source of the Mississippi River.

As a result of the new treaty, the Chippewa were placed on several small reservations. Hole-in-the-Day knew that they would have to learn to farm in order to survive. He decided to teach them by example. He became a farmer, clearing land, and plowing and planting fields. His efforts were successful. After putting aside a generous supply of vegetables to feed his own family during the winter, he had enough left to sell. He set another example by building his own frame house. In 1857, the Indian agent who lived with the Chippewa reported that the chief had done more for his "tribe than has ever been done by white men."

19

Hole-in-the-Day may have become a farmer, but he was still a warrior. When the Sioux killed eleven Chippewa, including a chief, he led the war party that avenged their deaths. Another group of Sioux dug up the grave of Hole-in-the-Day's father. Hole-in-the-Day and his men caught up to the Sioux and killed five of them. During this fight, Hole-in-the-Day was wounded in the leg. He took a stagecoach back to Crow Wing, the town closest to his farm. He was later called "a civilized barbarian who goes scalp hunting by stage."

Hole-in-the-Day usually managed to get along with the Indian agents sent by the government to supervise the Chippewa. But in 1861, a new agent, Lucius Walker, took charge of the Chippewa agency at Crow Wing. Hole-in-the-Day and some friends soon discovered that Walker was dishonest. When they got proof that Walker was keeping part of the money that was due to the Chippewa for the land they sold, Hole-in-the-Day tried to get him fired.

Hole-in-the-Day grew angry when the government took no action against Walker. In August 1862, the new Commissioner of Indian Affairs William Dole was in Minnesota to make a treaty with some other Indians who lived in the northwestern part of the state. Hole-in-the-Day decided to take drastic steps to make the commissioner take the complaints about Walker seriously. Hole-in-the-Day sent messages to the band chiefs telling them to join him in attacking the whites. The chiefs were cautious. They saw no reason to go to war. Their warriors killed some cattle and took a few whites prisoner. No one was killed, and the whites were soon released.

Agent Walker heard what was happening. He sent for troops from nearby Fort Ripley to arrest Hole-in-the-Day, but the chief avoided capture. Walker then abandoned the Indian agency. He fled south headed for St. Paul. He was so frightened, however, that he went insane and killed himself.

Commissioner Dole agreed to talk with Hole-in-the-Day. Dole arrived at Crow Wing on September 10 with one hundred soldiers. Hole-in-the-Day met him backed by one hundred of his warriors. The meeting was unsuccessful, and Dole decided to arrest the chief. He changed his mind when he learned that another group of Hole-in-the-Day's warriors had arrived and had surrounded the council ground. Badly outnumbered, Dole let the chief go free.

Dole returned to Washington, D.C., after instructing the Crow Wing postmaster to deal with Hole-in-the-Day. Meanwhile, two white men from Crow Wing had gone to Hole-in-the-Day's farm and burned down his house. The postmaster promised the chief that the government would pay for the house, but he refused to meet Hole-in-the-Day's other demands. As time went by with these issues still unsettled, the Chippewa began to desert their chief. Their support had been halfhearted at best. Hole-in-the-Day had all but given up when the Minnesota legislature came to his rescue.

By law, Indian matters were handled by the United States government. States were not supposed to interfere. In this case, however, the state took action. The Sioux had gone on the warpath in August. About five hundred settlers in southern Minnesota had been killed before the Sioux uprising was stopped. State officials didn't want war with the Chippewa, too. When it appeared that the federal officials could not control Hole-in-the-Day, the governor and some other state officials went to Crow Wing. On September 15, they made an agreement promising Hole-in-the-Day that the Chippewa would receive all the money to which they were entitled.

Hole-in-the-Day had won a minor victory, but his standing with both his people and the whites had been damaged. He had been a chief for fifteen years, and he was wealthy and famous. He had earned his money through hard work on his farm and from gifts that the government had given him for handling Chippewa affairs, but many Chippewa and whites were jealous of him. Some Chippewa thought he had been too friendly with the government.

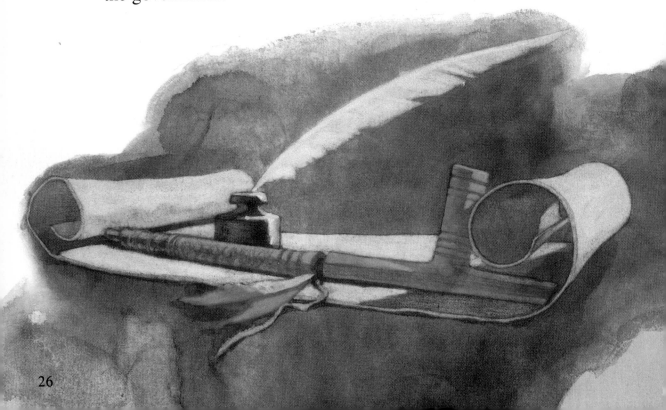

HOLE·IN·THE·DAY

In 1863, the government decided that all the Mississippi bands should move to one large reservation. Hole-in-the-Day did not help make the treaty that arranged for the move. The Chippewa did not like the treaty that the other leaders made. Once again the Chippewa turned to Hole-in-the-Day for help in dealing with the government. Over the next few years, he made three trips to Washington, D.C., trying to settle on a suitable place for the new reservation.

Between trips, Hole-in-the-Day started a new farm. With $5,000 he received from the government for the house that had been burned, he built and furnished a new home. In 1865, he enrolled one of his daughters in a boarding school in St. Paul. Unfortunately, during the following year he had a serious argument with some mixed-blood traders. The reason for the argument is unknown, but important men who had been his friends became his enemies.

Finally, a treaty establishing the White Earth Reservation was made in 1867. The government promised to set up farms and build houses, roads, and a sawmill for the Indians. Hole-in-the-Day also arranged for the treaty to state that no mixed-bloods would receive Indian money unless they lived at White Earth. The mixed-blood traders were upset about the treaty terms. They knew Hole-in-the Day intended to keep them off the reservation so they would not receive their money. They began to plot against him.

In 1868, the government wanted the Chippewa to move to the new reservation. No fields had been cleared or houses built, so Hole-in-the-Day told his people not to move until the work was done. He believed that the improvements would not be made once the Indians were on the reservation. Some Christian Chippewa, however, did not understand why he wanted to delay the move. Anxious to get away from the whiskey dealers in Crow Wing, they insisted on moving. When the mixed-blood traders saw that some Indians were going to White Earth, they took action to make sure they would be allowed on the reservation.

On June 27, 1868, Hole-in-the-Day was murdered by nine Indians hired by the traders. The chief and one of his cousins were riding in a buggy on the way to the Indian agency when the Indians stopped them and shot Hole-in-the-Day.

Many people thought that Hole-in-the-Day would always be famous as a great Indian leader. But most American Indian leaders who are remembered today were great warriors who challenged the might of the United States Army and who resisted the federal government. Hole-in-the-Day did neither. His military exploits came against the Sioux, and he led his tribe along a path of cooperation with the federal government. As a result, he was soon forgotten by the general public. As colorful and gifted as he was, he failed to capture lasting fame.

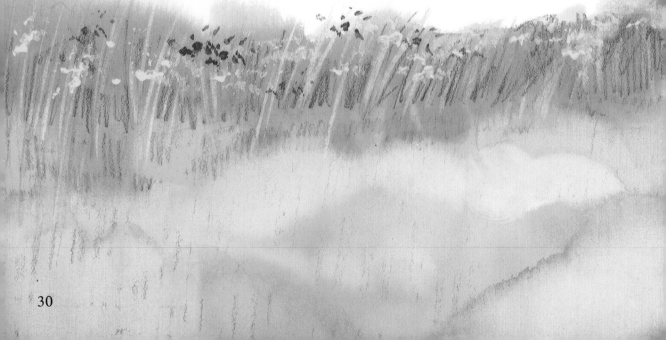

HISTORY OF HOLE-IN-THE-DAY

1820	Fort Snelling was established to protect white settlers and to keep the peace between the warring Chippewa and Sioux.
1828	Hole-in-the-Day was born. Andrew Jackson was elected president of the United States.
1830	Congress passed the Indian Removal Act which allowed the government to move the Eastern Indian tribes west of the Mississippi River.
1838	Hole-in-the-Day earned the right to wear his first eagle feather for killing an enemy.
1845	Texas was annexed to the United States and admitted to the Union.
1847	Hole-in-the-Day became head chief of the Mississippi Chippewa at age nineteen.
1848	Gold was discovered in California. The Treaty of Guadalupe Hidalgo ended the war with Mexico.
1855	Hole-in-the-Day went to Washington, D.C., where he agreed to a treaty ceding most of the Chippewa lands in Minnesota to the government.
1861-1865	The Civil War was fought. Abraham Lincoln was president.
1862	Hole-in-the-Day engineered an agreement with the government so that the Chippewa would receive money to which they were entitled.
1867	Hole-in-the-Day helped prepare a treaty establishing a new reservation and other benefits for the Chippewa.
1868	Hole-in-the-Day died. President Andrew Johnson was impeached.